My Manna for Today ☀

A Journal to Record the Faithfulness of God

Michelle Bader

My Manna for Today

How do you survive each day? What is it that gets you through? Do you rely on yourself, your strength, your power? In a world full of self-empowerment, it is easy to become entrapped in that thinking. If I just work harder, become stronger, believe more, than I will be able to conquer the day and survive.

At one time I was trapped in that way of thinking. I was believing that in my own power I could do anything. The problem lies in that I do not have the capability inside of me to survive even one second on my own. I am weak, I am human, and I cannot on my own provide what I need to sustain myself. Only the one who created me can give me what is needed, only He can provide in ways that I would never think of or imagine.

Now that I have tasted what God can do I know that it far exceeds anything I could do for myself. I have learned that in my darkest times, in my biggest storms only He knows what I need and can give it to me. In those times when I can barely keep my head above water I do not know what I need. In all His wisdom God can see what is above the water and on the distant shore. He dives down deep and rescues me. As I cough out the water that has started to permeate into my lungs He helps me breathe again.

His holy breath brings me to my knees. The peace he imparts to me cannot be explained in human words. As His power continues to fill me up, my lifeless body begins to gather strength and my heart begins to beat again. In His arms I find that in my weakness He is made strong.

I have learned that each day God gives me what I need. I have come to call this my manna. In the Bible it talks about when the Israelites wandering in the desert for 40 years. During this time the only way they could eat was to rely on the Manna that God sent from heaven. This food had to be gathered in the morning or it would melt. They were to gather only enough for that day. When they tried to gather more than a days supply it would go bad and be full of worms. Through this process they learned to rely on God each day for his provisions. (Exodus 16)

During my storms God has done the same thing for me. Sometimes He does it in physical ways and sometimes spiritual ways. Each day I pray "God please send me my manna today." Since praying that prayer, He has never failed me. He always gives me what I need to keep going. It could be a call from a friend, a verse or even a smile from a stranger. My expectations are often exceeded as I see the incredible manna he provides.

This journal is a place to record your personal manna, a place to reflect on the gifts that God gives you each and every day. This is more than a "positive journal" this is a way of not only pondering the many ways God provides for you but also as an act of worship and praise. On the pages I share the Manna that God has given me. I hope it demonstrates to you the faithfulness of God and helps you to look for Manna in the details of your life.

On these pages there is a place that you can record God's faithfulness for generations to come. You can refer back to this when you feel like you are drowning. You can share this with your family and remind them of God's faithfulness. As you look over the pages you can anticipate the things that God will show you through this manna journey. Manna is there every day, you just have to look for it. Somedays it will be easier to spot than others. This journal is designed to only take a few minutes a day. Each page has space for two entries, I do not want this to be another thing on your never ending to do list, but something you look forward to and know that it only needs to be a sentence or two.

It is designed to quickly record your manna and refer to in the future. I challenge you to challenge yourself to record your manna for 30 days. After this time, I am sure you will look over what God has done and continue to journal. During your journaling, I pray that you can see His hand on your life. I pray that this journal transforms and renews your belief in the power and love of Jesus.

this Journal Belongs to

_____

Journal Start Date

_____

Today's Manna was about something that didn't happen. While in the school parking lot I came VERY close to backing into another car. Thank you God for the Manna of NOT getting in an accident!

My Manna for Today ☀

_____

_____

_____

_____

_____

_____

My Manna for Today ☀

_____

_____

_____

_____

_____

_____

Am I looking for the little Manna as well as the big Manna?

My Manna for Today ☀

_____

_____

_____

_____

_____

_____

My Manna for Today ☀

_____

_____

_____

_____

_____

_____

My Manna came in an unusual way today. I woke up to my kids telling me to come into the yard. On the yard were many colored Easter eggs, three Easter baskets, and gift cards. On the door was a sign that said, "You've been egged" What a fun gift!

My Manna for Today ☀

_____

_____

_____

_____

_____

_____

My Manna for Today ☀

_____

_____

_____

_____

_____

_____

man·na /noun (in the Bible) the substance miraculously supplied as food to the Israelites in the wilderness (Exod. 16). ** an unexpected or gratuitous benefit

My Manna for Today ☀

_____

_____

_____

_____

_____

_____

My Manna for Today ☀

_____

_____

_____

_____

_____

_____

_____

Today my Manna is was writing these words "This is the day that the Lord has made. I will rejoice and be glad in it. I will press on, I will be still. I know God is for me. I know God longs to be gracious to me. I know He will make beauty out of all of these ashes, for this is the day that the Lord has made,"

My Manna for Today ☼

_____

_____

_____

_____

_____

_____

_____

My Manna for Today ☼

_____

_____

_____

_____

_____

_____

_____

_____

"Feeling gratitude and not expressing it is like wrapping a present and not giving it." - William Arthur Ward

My Manna for Today ☀

_____

_____

_____

_____

_____

_____

My Manna for Today ☀

_____

_____

_____

_____

_____

_____

Today at church a woman I never met came up to me and said, "I feel like God wants me to tell you that He is so proud of you." I received this news during my husband's cancer battle and that meant more than she could ever know.

My Manna for Today ☀

_____

_____

_____

_____

_____

_____

My Manna for Today ☀

_____

_____

_____

_____

_____

_____

"I am even thankful for the negative things that have made me a stronger and better person." -Joanna Krupa

My Manna for Today ☀

_____

_____

_____

_____

_____

_____

My Manna for Today ☀

_____

_____

_____

_____

_____

_____

_____

Today God sent me Manna in a form of a verse. Exodus 14:14 "The Lord will fight for you, you need only to be still" (NIV) Those words were exactly what I needed to hear during a very rocky storm.

My Manna for Today ☀

_____

_____

_____

_____

_____

_____

My Manna for Today ☀

_____

_____

_____

_____

_____

_____

_____

_____

"Today my Manna was a beautiful sunny day to take the kids on an adventure to the lake!

My Manna for Today ☀

_____

_____

_____

_____

_____

_____

My Manna for Today ☀

_____

_____

_____

_____

_____

_____

_____

_____

"There's no happier person than a truly thankful, content person." -Joyce Meyer

My Manna for Today ☀

_____

_____

_____

_____

_____

_____

My Manna for Today ☀

_____

_____

_____

_____

_____

_____

_____

Because of my husband's cancer we are not able to have people over very often. My daughter wanted to have a slumber party for her 12th Birthday. Amazingly enough God provided a way for us to have 13 girls spend the night at a beautiful house with a pool. Thank you God for this Manna!

My Manna for Today ☀

_____

_____

_____

_____

_____

_____

My Manna for Today ☀

_____

_____

_____

_____

_____

_____

"I know that when I pray, something wonderful happens. Not just to the person or persons for whom I'm praying, but also something wonderful happens to me. I'm grateful that I'm heard." - Maya Angelou

My Manna for Today ☼

_____
_____
_____
_____
_____
_____

My Manna for Today ☼

_____
_____
_____
_____
_____
_____

Last night my Manna was cuddling with my husband, laying my head on his chest and hearing the beat of his heart. A beat that reminds me of the gift of time, the gift of another moment another day another month to be fully present and never take for granted one single heartbeat.

My Manna for Today ☀

_____

_____

_____

_____

_____

_____

My Manna for Today ☀

_____

_____

_____

_____

_____

_____

_____

_____

"Keep your eyes open to your mercies. The man who forgets to be thankful has fallen asleep in life." - Robert Louis Stevenson

My Manna for Today ☀

_____

_____

_____

_____

_____

_____

My Manna for Today ☀

_____

_____

_____

_____

_____

_____

_____

Manna can come in the form of angels on earth. At a time that my husband was very sick, and money was very tight a group of people that I didn't even know came together and got everything on my kids Christmas wish list. It was a beautiful Christmas!

My Manna for Today ☀

_____

_____

_____

_____

_____

_____

_____

My Manna for Today ☀

_____

_____

_____

_____

_____

_____

_____

_____

Before I get out of bed, I am saying thank you. I know how important it is to be thankful." -Al Jarreau

My Manna for Today ☀

_____

_____

_____

_____

_____

_____

My Manna for Today ☀

_____

_____

_____

_____

_____

_____

_____

Today my beautiful and simple Manna came in the form of an email from my son's teacher telling me how well he was doing. Sometimes Manna is the seemingly small things.

Manna for Today ☀

_____

_____

_____

_____

_____

_____

My Manna for Today ☀

_____

_____

_____

_____

_____

_____

_____

_____

"If you are really thankful, what do you do? You share." – W. Clement Stone

My Manna for Today ☀

_____

_____

_____

_____

_____

_____

My Manna for Today ☀

_____

_____

_____

_____

_____

_____

_____

When praying today I felt the peace of God cover my entire body as I heard the words "Be Still". I was reminded of the words from Psalm 37:7a "Be still, be patient, wait for the Lord to act"

My Manna for Today ☀

_____

_____

_____

_____

_____

_____

My Manna for Today ☀

_____

_____

_____

_____

_____

_____

I've started to look at life differently. When you're thanking God for every little you – every meal, every time you wake up, every time you take a sip of water – you can't help but be more thankful for life itself, for the unlikely and miraculous fact that you exist at all." – A.J. Jacobs

My Manna for Today ☼

My Manna for Today ☼

"Today my Manna came while seeing my very ill husband playing basketball with my boys. It was an amazing sight and great memory for them!

My Manna for Today ☀

My Manna for Today ☀

"When I started counting my blessings, my whole life turned around>" – Willie Nelson

My Manna for Today ☀

_____

_____

_____

_____

_____

_____

_____

My Manna for Today ☀

_____

_____

_____

_____

_____

_____

_____

Manna can come in the form of money! As my husband and I continue down his cancer battle money is really tight. Today we found an anonymous envelope at the door with $1,000 in cash! Talk about God raining down the money right when needed!

My Manna for Today ☀

_____

_____

_____

_____

_____

_____

My Manna for Today ☀

_____

_____

_____

_____

_____

_____

_____

"Be true to yourself, help others, make each day your masterpiece, make friendship a fine art, drink deeply from good books – especially the Bible, build a shelter against a rainy day, give thanks for your blessings and pray for guidance every day." – John Wooden

My Manna for Today ☼

_____

_____

_____

_____

_____

_____

_____

My Manna for Today ☼

_____

_____

_____

_____

_____

_____

_____

Crying in the car today I turned on the radio and the song was exactly what I needed to hear. Such sweet Manna!

My Manna for Today ☀

_____

_____

_____

_____

_____

_____

My Manna for Today ☀

_____

_____

_____

_____

_____

_____

"Make it a habit to tell people thank you. To express your appreciation, sincerely and without the expectation of anything in return. Truly appreciate those around you, and you'll soon find many others around you. Truly appreciate life, and you'll find that you have more of it." – Ralph Marston

My Manna for Today ☀

_____

_____

_____

_____

_____

_____

_____

My Manna for Today ☀

_____

_____

_____

_____

_____

_____

_____

Sitting in the carpool line today a message popped up on my phone from an acquaintance on FB. She told me that seeing me going through hard trials has inspired her to persevere through her own hard times.

My Manna for Today ☀

_____

_____

_____

_____

_____

_____

My Manna for Today ☀

_____

_____

_____

_____

_____

_____

_____

"The real gift of gratitude is that the more grateful you are, the more present you become." -Robert Holden

My Manna for Today ☀

_____

_____

_____

_____

_____

_____

_____

My Manna for Today ☀

_____

_____

_____

_____

_____

_____

_____

During my prayer time today, all of the sudden the words "My grace is sufficient for you" came into my mind. I looked it up and found the rest of the verse that said, "In your weakness, I am made strong" Wow, what perfect Manna for me today in my weakened state!

My Manna for Today ☀

_____

_____

_____

_____

_____

_____

_____

My Manna for Today ☀

_____

_____

_____

_____

_____

_____

_____

"Gratitude can transform common days into thanksgiving, turn routine jobs into joy and change ordinary opportunities into blessings." -William Arthur Ward

My Manna for Today ☀

_____

_____

_____

_____

_____

_____

My Manna for Today ☀

_____

_____

_____

_____

_____

_____

Small, but big to this Mama's heart- my boys cleaned their room on their own and didn't complain! God's Manna is so good!

My Manna for Today ☀

_____

_____

_____

_____

_____

_____

My Manna for Today ☀

_____

_____

_____

_____

_____

_____

"Develop an attitude of gratitude and give thanks for everything that happens to you, knowing that every step forward is a step toward achieving something bigger and better than your current situation." -Brian Tracy

My Manna for Today ☀

_____

_____

_____

_____

_____

_____

_____

My Manna for Today ☀

_____

_____

_____

_____

_____

_____

_____

Today my Manna was from my student's, they left notes all over my desk saying how much they love me.

My Manna for Today ☀

_____

_____

_____

_____

_____

_____

_____

My Manna for Today ☀

_____

_____

_____

_____

_____

_____

_____

"God has promised to supply all our needs. What we don't have now, we don't need now." –Elizabeth Elliot

My Manna for Today ☼

_____

_____

_____

_____

_____

_____

My Manna for Today ☼

_____

_____

_____

_____

_____

_____

Wow, so thankful for God's protective Manna! Today the kids and I began sliding on ice and ended up on the wrong side of the road facing the wrong way! So thankful that no other cars were on the road and that we came away unharmed!

My Manna for Today ☀

_____

_____

_____

_____

_____

_____

My Manna for Today ☀

_____

_____

_____

_____

_____

_____

"If I succeed, I will give thanks. If I fail, I will seek His grace." –Max Lucado

My Manna for Today ☀

_____

_____

_____

_____

_____

_____

My Manna for Today ☀

_____

_____

_____

_____

_____

_____

Today my family was at the beach and wanted to fulfill my husband's dream of riding in a helicopter. Last night the helicopter company called my family and said we wouldn't be able to go due to the weather. It was a miracle, we woke up today to sunny skies and were able to go up in the helicopter! "

My Manna for Today ☀

_____

_____

_____

_____

_____

_____

My Manna for Today ☀

_____

_____

_____

_____

_____

_____

God is in control, and therefore in EVERYTHING I can give thanks - not because of the situation but because of the One who directs and rules over it." –Kay Arthur

My Manna for Today ☀

_____

_____

_____

_____

_____

_____

My Manna for Today ☀

_____

_____

_____

_____

_____

_____

Best Manna ever! My husband's cancer did NOT grow since his last scan! I can finally breathe a little!

My Manna for Today ☀

_____

_____

_____

_____

_____

_____

My Manna for Today ☀

_____

_____

_____

_____

_____

_____

"In happy moments, PRAISE GOD. In difficult moments, SEEK GOD. In quiet moments, WORSHIP GOD. In painful moments, TRUST GOD. Every moment, THANK GOD." –Rick Warren

My Manna for Today ☀

_____

_____

_____

_____

_____

_____

_____

My Manna for Today ☀

_____

_____

_____

_____

_____

_____

_____

Awesome Manna! I got the teaching job I have always wanted! I will be working with small groups of students helping them improve math and reading!

My Manna for Today ☀

_____

_____

_____

_____

_____

_____

My Manna for Today ☀

_____

_____

_____

_____

_____

_____

"I have held many things in my hands, and I have lost them all; but whatever I have placed in God's hands, that, I still possess." –Corrie ten Boom

My Manna for Today ☀

_____

_____

_____

_____

_____

_____

_____

My Manna for Today ☀

_____

_____

_____

_____

_____

_____

_____

Today my Manna is my husband's life. He lost over half of his body weight in blood, but thanks to a blood transfusion he is still alive!

My Manna for Today ☀

_____

_____

_____

_____

_____

_____

My Manna for Today ☀

_____

_____

_____

_____

_____

_____

It's one thing to be grateful. It's another to give thanks. Gratitude is what you feel. Thanksgiving is what you do." –Tim Keller

My Manna for Today ☀

_____

_____

_____

_____

_____

_____

My Manna for Today ☀

_____

_____

_____

_____

_____

_____

Today I was crying a deep heart wrenching cry. I cried out "God, please send my Manna today" at that exact moment I looked at my phone and had a message from a friend I hadn't heard from in a while that said, "Just thinking about you" WOW, God is so good!

My Manna for Today ☀

_____

_____

_____

_____

_____

_____

_____

My Manna for Today ☀

_____

_____

_____

_____

_____

_____

_____

"When we choose thankful prayer over wallowing in anxiety and worry, we are demonstrating an unwavering trust in God." –Priscilla Shirer

My Manna for Today ☀

_____

_____

_____

_____

_____

_____

_____

My Manna for Today ☀

_____

_____

_____

_____

_____

_____

_____

Today in the sunny backyard my daughter and I made dandelion chain crowns. The warmth of the sun, her smile and the bright yellow flowers reminded me of how much God loves me!

My Manna for Today ☀

_____

_____

_____

_____

_____

_____

My Manna for Today ☀

_____

_____

_____

_____

_____

_____

"Gratitude produces deep, abiding joy because we know that God is working in us, even through difficulties." –Charles Stanley

My Manna for Today ☀

_____

_____

_____

_____

_____

_____

My Manna for Today ☀

_____

_____

_____

_____

_____

_____

My Manna came today when my husband was feeling unusually well after chemo and he took me out to dinner!

My Manna for today ☀

_____

_____

_____

_____

_____

My Manna for today ☀

_____

_____

_____

_____

_____

_____

"If there was ever a secret for unleashing God's powerful peace in a situation, it's developing a heart of true thanksgiving." –Lysa Terkeurst

My Manna for Today ☀

_____

_____

_____

_____

_____

_____

_____

My Manna for Today ☀

_____

_____

_____

_____

_____

_____

_____

Today my Manna came when my mom shared this verse with me "The Lord is close to the brokenhearted and saves those who are crushed in spirit" Psalm 34:18

My Manna for Today ☀

_____

_____

_____

_____

_____

_____

_____

My Manna for Today ☀

_____

_____

_____

_____

_____

_____

_____

"To be grateful is to recognize the love of God in everything He has given us --
and He has given us everything. Every breath we draw is a gift of His love,
every moment of existence is a grace, for it brings with its immense graces
from Him." –Thomas Merton

My Manna for Today ☀

_____

_____

_____

_____

_____

_____

_____

My Manna for Today ☀

_____

_____

_____

_____

_____

_____

_____

My manna today is my tribe of friends and family who daily pray for me. I know they are there for me any time I need them!

My Manna for Today ☀

_____

_____

_____

_____

_____

My Manna for Today ☀

_____

_____

_____

_____

_____

_____

"The Sun you created is shining brightly under your command. The birds you set into the air chirp about your splendor. The flowers dance for joy at your greatness. And I have nothing more than a grateful heart to offer to you Oh Lord my God! Thank you for creating me." -Norman Jagger

My Manna for Today ☀

_____

_____

_____

_____

_____

_____

My Manna for Today ☀

_____

_____

_____

_____

_____

_____

_____

My Manna appeared to be in the form of a dream. I asked God to show me what would happen to my husband during his cancer battle. In my dream I was walking on the ocean and I began to sink, I was underwater when Jesus reached out his hand to me and said "Trust Me" and lifted me up. What a good reminder to trust Him at all times!

My Manna for Today ☀

_____

_____

_____

_____

_____

_____

My Manna for Today ☀

_____

_____

_____

_____

_____

_____

_____

"Gratitude develops faith. The surest path out of a slump is marked by the road sign "thank you, God."" -Max Lucado

My Manna for Today ☀

_____

_____

_____

_____

_____

_____

My Manna for Today ☀

_____

_____

_____

_____

_____

_____

_____

My Manna came in the mail today! I found a card with gift cards in it for Applebees. A woman I never met sent them to me because she saw on Facebook that my husband and I went there on a date and wanted to send us back. What a great piece of Manna today!

My Manna for Today ☀

_____

_____

_____

_____

_____

_____

_____

My Manna for Today ☀

_____

_____

_____

_____

_____

_____

_____

"I have lived to thank God that all my prayers have not been answered." -Jean Ingelow

My Manna for Today ☀

_____

_____

_____

_____

_____

_____

My Manna for Today ☀

_____

_____

_____

_____

_____

_____

_____

My Manna today was again a display of God's love. I was getting worried about my husband's cancer and looking things up on the internet on my phone when suddenly I was interrupted by a friend texting me a worship song and saying "This made me think of you" Wow, I shut off the search and listened to the song!

My Manna for Today ☀

_____

_____

_____

_____

_____

_____

My Manna for Today ☀

_____

_____

_____

_____

_____

_____

_____

"I wake up every morning to say thank you God for waking me up to see another day to enjoy life."- Michael Myers Jr

My Manna for Today ☀

_____

_____

_____

_____

_____

_____

My Manna for Today ☀

_____

_____

_____

_____

_____

_____

My Manna came in the form of a call today. A woman I didn't know said she had been hired by an anonymous person to clean my house several times. How awesome it that?

My Manna for Today ☀

_____

_____

_____

_____

_____

_____

My Manna for Today ☀

_____

_____

_____

_____

_____

_____

The best way to say, I love you God is to live your life doing your best. The best way to say, "Thank you, God," is by letting go of the past and living in the present moment, right here and now."-Miguel Angel Ruiz

My Manna for Today ☀

_____

_____

_____

_____

_____

_____

My Manna for Today ☀

_____

_____

_____

_____

_____

_____

_____

My Manna today was a gentle reminder from God, I thought about how I can be Manna to someone else today. I have begun looking for more opportunities to do this!

My Manna for Today ☀

_____

_____

_____

_____

_____

_____

My Manna for Today ☀

_____

_____

_____

_____

_____

_____

_____

_____

"On my bad days I seek you, on my good days I thank you, on my great days I praise you, but every day I need you, Thank you God for always being here for me." - Rashida Rowe

My Manna for Today ☀

_____

_____

_____

_____

_____

_____

_____

My Manna for Today ☀

_____

_____

_____

_____

_____

_____

_____

I love the Manna verses God gives me! Here is the one for today! Isaiah 30:14 "Yet the Lord longs to be gracious to you, therefore He will rise up to show compassion. For the Lord is a God of justice. Blessed are all who wait for him!"

My Manna for Today ☀

_____

_____

_____

_____

_____

_____

My Manna for Today ☀

_____

_____

_____

_____

_____

_____

"Every morning is a gift from the almighty God. Before you think about anything else remember that life comes from the one above and thank him for all that he blesses us with." -Kim Bathers

My Manna for Today

_____

_____

_____

_____

_____

_____

My Manna for Today

_____

_____

_____

_____

_____

_____

My Manna was a butterfly today, actually two of them! I randomly saw them flutter by me at random times which reminded me that God is transforming me into a beautiful butterfly during these hard times.

My Manna for Today ☀

_____

_____

_____

_____

_____

_____

My Manna for Today ☀

_____

_____

_____

_____

_____

_____

Whatever happens in your life, no matter how troubling things might seem, do not enter the neighborhood of despair. Even when all doors remain closed, God will open up a new path only for you. Be thankful!" -Elif Shafak

My Manna for Today ☀

_____

_____

_____

_____

_____

_____

_____

My Manna for Today ☀

_____

_____

_____

_____

_____

_____

_____

"My tire went flat today. The Manna was that I was at my kids' school and not all alone. The principal of the school came out to help me, so thankful for that Manna today!

My Manna for Today ☀

_____

_____

_____

_____

_____

_____

My Manna for Today ☀

_____

_____

_____

_____

_____

_____

"We would worry less if we praised more. Thanksgiving is the enemy of discontent and dissatisfaction."- Harry Ironside

My Manna for Today ☀

My Manna for Today ☀

My Manna today is that I didn't lose my eyesight! I ended up in the ER because of some pool chemicals that flew in my eyes. I was told I could lose my sight, so thankful I didn't!!

My Manna for Today ☀

_____

_____

_____

_____

_____

_____

My Manna for Today ☀

_____

_____

_____

_____

_____

_____

"Let us thank God heartily as often as we pray that we have His Spirit in us to teach us to pray. Thanksgiving will draw our hearts out to God and keep us engaged with Him; it will take our attention from ourselves and give the Spirit room in our hearts."- Andrew Murray

My Manna for Today ☀

_____

_____

_____

_____

_____

_____

_____

My Manna for Today ☀

_____

_____

_____

_____

_____

_____

_____

Such fun Manna! Today my kids and I found over 100 unbroken sand dollars at the beach! They are so beautiful!

My Manna for Today ☀

_____

_____

_____

_____

_____

_____

_____

_____

My Manna for Today ☀

_____

_____

_____

_____

_____

_____

_____

_____

"God wants to see prayers that are filled with genuine praise and thanksgiving for what He has done in the past. He wants our hearts to be filled with awe and gratitude for His blessings. He wants us to set up memorials in our hearts testifying to the provisions He has given us."- Michael Youssef

My Manna for Today ☀

_____

_____

_____

_____

_____

_____

My Manna for Today ☀

_____

_____

_____

_____

_____

_____

_____

My Manna showed up today in flowers at my door. It is the first day of my husband's chemo and this little piece of love helped me get through.

My Manna for Today ☀
_____
_____
_____
_____
_____
_____
_____

My Manna for Today ☀
_____
_____
_____
_____
_____
_____
_____

"Yes, give thanks for "all things" for, as it has been well said "Our disappointments are but His appointments."- A. W. Pink

My Manna for Today ☀

_____

_____

_____

_____

_____

_____

My Manna for Today ☀

_____

_____

_____

_____

_____

_____

_____

My Manna today was the strength God gave me to get out of bed. He reminded me of my blessings and helped me to focus on those.

My Manna for Today ☀

_____

_____

_____

_____

_____

_____

My Manna for Today ☀

_____

_____

_____

_____

_____

_____

"A state of mind that sees God in everything is evidence of growth in grace and a thankful heart."- Charles Finney

My Manna for Today ☀

My Manna for Today ☀

Today I watched a sermon that spoke deeply to my heart from Elevation Church. Pastor Steven said, "If God allowed it, I can accept it." Those words changed my perspective!

My Manna for Today ☀

_____

_____

_____

_____

_____

_____

My Manna for Today ☀

_____

_____

_____

_____

_____

_____

"The thankful heart sees the best part of every situation. It sees problems and weaknesses as opportunities, struggles as refining tools, and sinners as saints in progress." - Francis Frangipane

My Manna for Today ☀

_____

_____

_____

_____

_____

_____

My Manna for Today ☀

_____

_____

_____

_____

_____

_____

Manna came in the form of a song playing over and over throughout the night in my mind. The chorus said "There's no wall you won't kick down, lie you won't tear down coming after me" It was God's way of saying he won't let me go, he will keep pursuing me.

My Manna for Today ☀

_____

_____

_____

_____

_____

_____

My Manna for Today ☀

_____

_____

_____

_____

_____

_____

_____

"Our God is not made of stone. His heart is the most sensitive and tender of all. No act goes unnoticed, no matter how insignificant or small. A cup of cold water is enough to put tears in the eyes of God. God celebrates our feeble expressions of gratitude." - Richard J. Foste

My Manna for Today ☀

_____

_____

_____

_____

_____

_____

My Manna for Today ☀

_____

_____

_____

_____

_____

_____

Today was a crazy morning as usual. I went to grab my keys and there was a note from my husband that said, "Thank you for always driving the kids to school." It was so nice to be appreciated!

My Manna for Today ☀

_____

_____

_____

_____

_____

_____

My Manna for Today ☀

_____

_____

_____

_____

_____

_____

"Gratitude changes the pangs of memory into a tranquil joy."- Dietrich Bonhoeffer

My Manna for Today ☀

_____

_____

_____

_____

_____

_____

My Manna for Today ☀

_____

_____

_____

_____

_____

_____

Today my Manna was simple and sweet. My son came home from his first day of school in 1st Grade and told me he made a new best friend!

My Manna for Today ☀

_____

_____

_____

_____

_____

_____

My Manna for Today ☀

_____

_____

_____

_____

_____

_____

."Keep your face to the sunshine and you cannot see a shadow." - Helen Keller

My Manna for Today ☀

_____

_____

_____

_____

_____

_____

My Manna for Today ☀

_____

_____

_____

_____

_____

_____

I met a new friend today. Even as an adult I like to make new friends and find someone to share life with! Manna all around!

My Manna for Today ☀

_____

_____

_____

_____

_____

_____

_____

My Manna for Today ☀

_____

_____

_____

_____

_____

_____

_____

"God is in control, and therefore in EVERYTHING I can give thanks - not because of the situation but because of the One who directs and rules over it."- Kay Arthur

My Manna for Today ☀

_____

_____

_____

_____

_____

_____

My Manna for Today ☀

_____

_____

_____

_____

_____

_____

_____

Today I prayed that God would show me a book to read. At the library my eyes were directed to the book "Through the Eyes of a Lion" by Levi Lusko. It ended up speaking to me so deeply and then I passed it on to my mom who passed it on to others.

My Manna for Today ☀

_____

_____

_____

_____

_____

_____

My Manna for Today ☀

_____

_____

_____

_____

_____

_____

"The Bible tells us that whenever we come before God, whatever our purpose or prayer request, we are always to come with a thankful heart."- David Jeremiah

My Manna for Today ☀

_____

_____

_____

_____

_____

_____

_____

My Manna for Today ☀

_____

_____

_____

_____

_____

_____

_____

Today my manna was a beautiful sunset, the beauty of God's creation reminds me of his love and faithfulness to me.

My Manna for Today ☀

_____

_____

_____

_____

_____

_____

My Manna for Today ☀

_____

_____

_____

_____

_____

_____

_____

"A state of mind that sees God in everything is evidence of growth in grace and a thankful heart." -G.K. Chesterton

My Manna for Today ☀

_____

_____

_____

_____

_____

_____

My Manna for Today ☀

_____

_____

_____

_____

_____

_____

My Manna came today when I was walking into my husband's scan to see if his cancer had grown. While walking in I saw some birds above and I was reminded that God cares for me even more than the birds and that I shouldn't worry!

My Manna for Today ☀

_____

_____

_____

_____

_____

_____

My Manna for Today ☀

_____

_____

_____

_____

_____

_____

The Christian who walks with the Lord and keeps constant communion with Him will see many reasons for rejoicing and thanksgiving all day long. -Charles Finney

My Manna for Today ☀

_____

_____

_____

_____

_____

_____

My Manna for Today ☀

_____

_____

_____

_____

_____

_____

Manna is all around today! Throughout the day God showed me through a variety of people how much he cares for me.

My Manna for Today ☀

_____

_____

_____

_____

_____

_____

My Manna for Today ☀

_____

_____

_____

_____

_____

_____

_____

"It's possible to be thankful wherever you find yourself. David Jeremiah

My Manna for Today ☀

_____

_____

_____

_____

_____

_____

My Manna for Today ☀

_____

_____

_____

_____

_____

_____

Feeling gratitude isn't born in us - it's something we are taught, and in turn, we teach our children."- Joyce Brother

My Manna for Today ☀

_____
_____
_____
_____
_____
_____

My Manna for Today ☀

_____
_____
_____
_____
_____
_____
_____
_____

God sent me Manna today while I was running. A fellow runner was running the opposite direction of me as he stuck out his hand to his side and gave me a high five with an encouraging smile. This simple gesture felt like God saying "You got this my girl, I am proud of you and cheering you on every day."

My Manna for Today ☼

_____

_____

_____

_____

_____

_____

My Manna for Today ☼

_____

_____

_____

_____

_____

_____

_____

How Can I be Manna to someone else today?

My Manna for Today ☼

_____

_____

_____

_____

_____

_____

My Manna for Today ☼

_____

_____

_____

_____

_____

_____

About the Author

Michelle Bader is a passionate writer, teacher and speaker. She lives in Vancouver, WA with her husband Luke and three kids, Hayden, Hayley and Payton. She recently published her true life story *Cancer Can't Crush Us -A Journey Through Strength, Love and Faith.* She loves spending time with friends and enjoying time with her family in the outdoors.

Michelle loves using the trials she has endured to help others and point them to God. She loves leading teams of people and speaking into people's lives.

If you would like to book her for a speaking engagement, please email her at inspire@michellebader.com

14068086R00060

Made in the USA
San Bernardino, CA
14 December 2018